T0056017

LINDSEY STIRLING
PIANO COLLECTION

Cover photo courtesy of Devin Graham

ISBN 978-1-5400-4114-2

Visit Hal Leonard Online at
www.halleonard.com

Contact Us:
Hal Leonard
7777 West Bluemound Road
Milwaukee, WI 53213
Email: info@halleonard.com

In Europe contact:
Hal Leonard Europe Limited
42 Wigmore Street
Marylebone, London, W1U 2RN
Email: info@halleonardeurope.com

In Australia contact:
Hal Leonard Australia Pty. Ltd.
4 Lentara Court
Cheltenham, Victoria, 3192 Australia
Email: info@halleonard.com.au

BEYOND THE VEIL

By LINDSEY STIRLING
and MARK MAXWELL
Arranged by David Russell

Powerfully ($\bullet$ = 65)

To Coda ⊕

D.S. al Coda

FIRST LIGHT

By LINDSEY STIRLING
and JAMES WONG
Arranged by David Russell

CRYSTALLIZE

By LINDSEY STIRLING
and MARKO GLOGOLJA
Arranged by David Russell

With fragility ($\quarternote$ = 70)

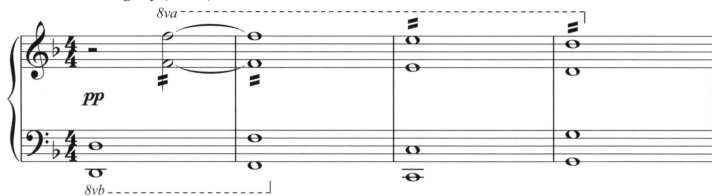

ELECTRIC DAISY VIOLIN

By LINDSEY STIRLING
and MARKO GLOGOLJA
Arranged by David Russell

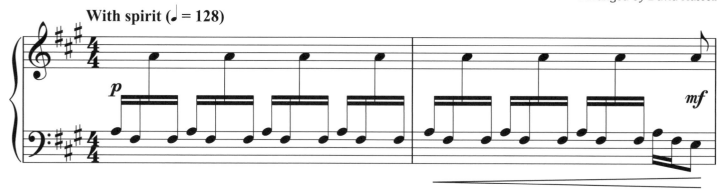

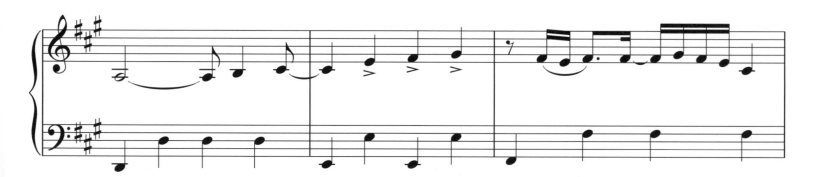

ELEMENTS

By LINDSEY STIRLING
and MARKO GLOGOLJA
Arranged by David Russell

With energy! (♩ = 140)

MOON TRANCE

Words and Music by LINDSEY STIRLING,
TAL MELTZER and PHILIP PATTERSON
Arranged by David Russell

ROUNDTABLE RIVAL

Words and Music by LINDSEY STIRLING,
BRANDON LOWRY and SCOTT GOLDSTONE
Arranged by David Russell

Country Rock (♩ = 127)

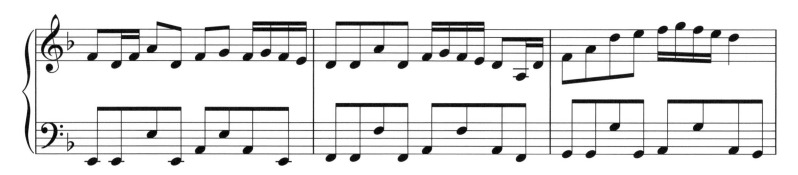

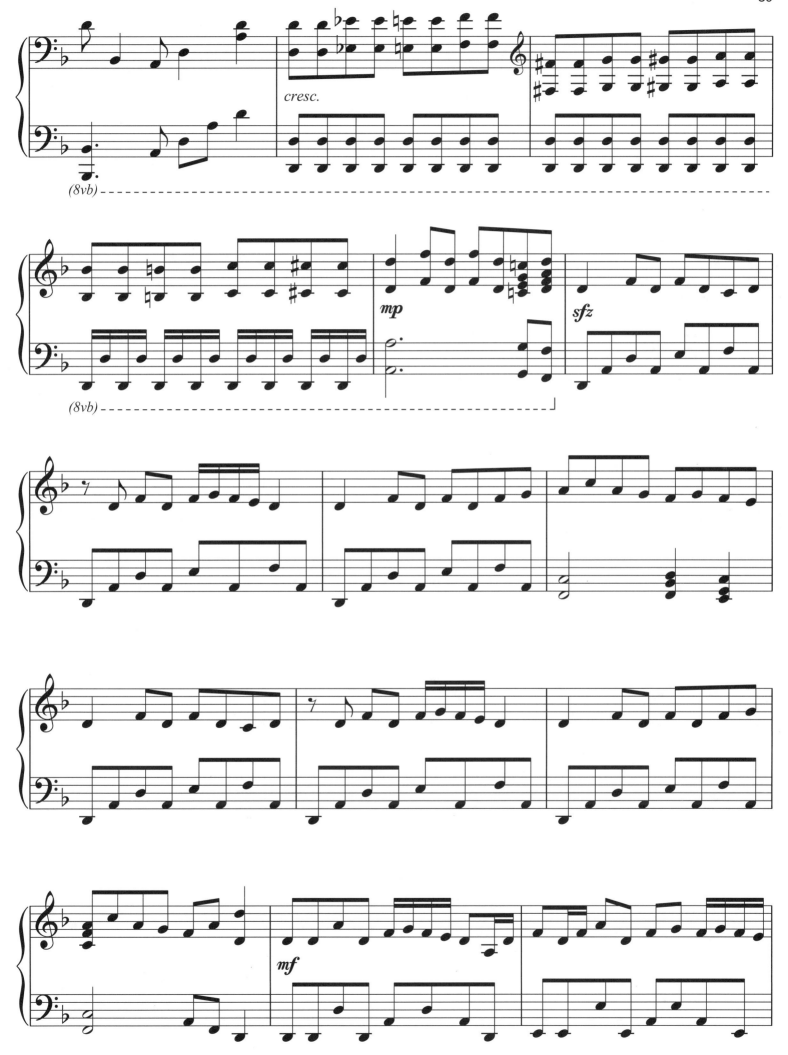

PRISM

Words and Music by LINDSEY STIRLING
and ROBERT DeLONG
Arranged by David Russell

SHATTER ME

Words and Music by DIA FRAMPTON,
MARK MAXWELL and LINDSEY STIRLING
Arranged by David Russell

SOMETHING WILD
from PETE'S DRAGON

Words and Music by LINDSEY STIRLING,
ANDREW McMAHON, PETER HANNA
and TAYLOR BIRD
Arranged by David Russell

SONG OF THE CAGED BIRD

By LINDSEY STIRLING
and MARKO GLOGOLJA
Arranged by David Russell

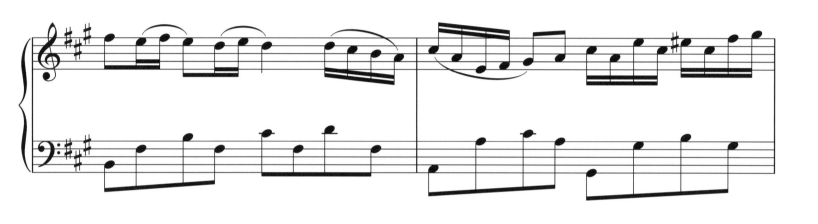

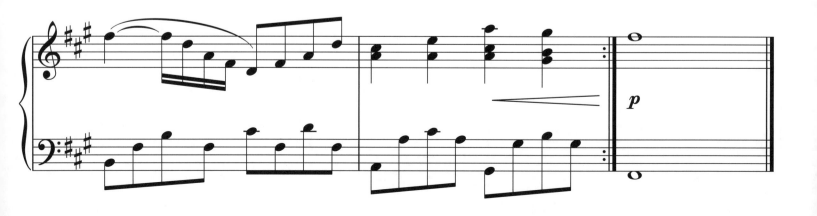

SPONTANEOUS ME

By LINDSEY STIRLING
and MARKO GLOGOLJA
Arranged by David Russell

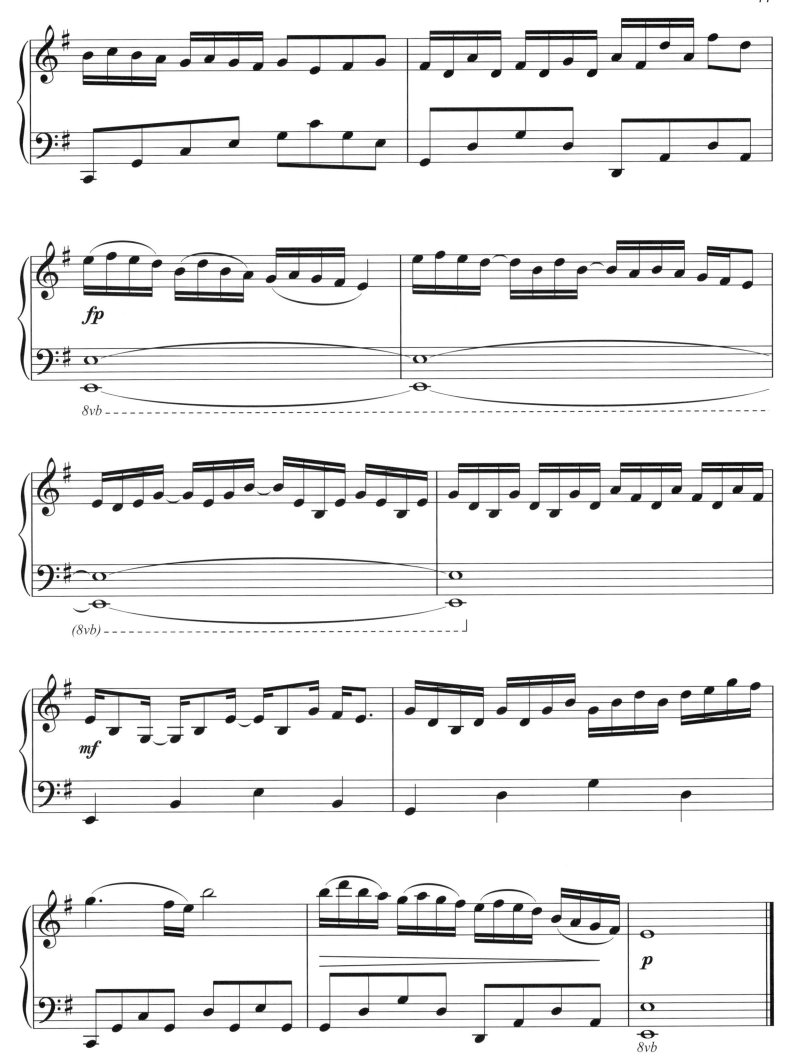

STAMPEDE

Words and Music by MARK BALLAS,
LINDSEY STIRLING and BRITTANY JEAN CARLSON
Arranged by David Russell

D.S. al Coda

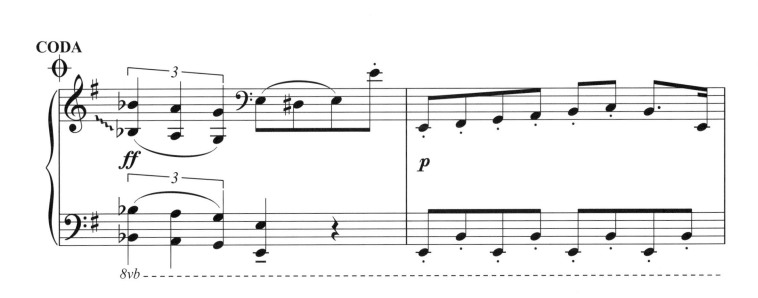

CODA

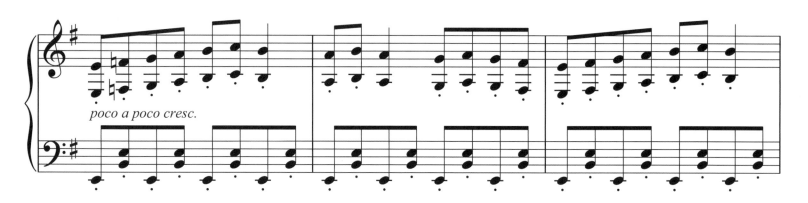

poco a poco cresc.

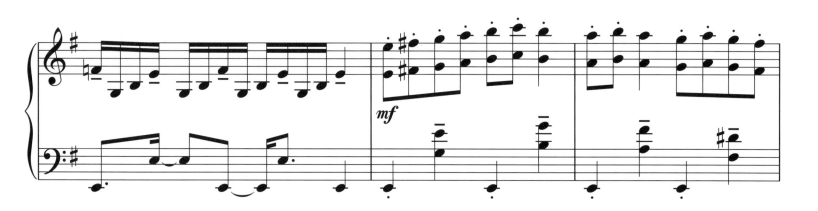

mf

f

ZI-ZI'S JOURNEY

By LINDSEY STIRLING
and AFSHIN SALMANI
Arranged by David Russell

To Coda ⊕

89

SUN SKIP

Words and Music by LINDSEY STIRLING
and ROBERT DeLONG
Arranged by David Russell